RECIPE SHORTS

DELICIOUS DISHES IN 140 CHARACTERS

PHOTOGRAPHY BY

Faith Mason

Kyle Books

Published in 2017 by Kyle Books
www.kylebooks.com

Distributed by National Book Network
4501 Forbes Blvd, Suite 200,
Lanham, MD 20706
Phone: (800) 462-6420
Fax: (800) 338-4550
customercare@nbnbooks.com

First published in Great Britain in 2017 by
Kyle Books, an imprint of Kyle Cathie Ltd

10 9 8 7 6 5 4 3 2 1

ISBN 978-1-909-487-66-6

DESIGN DIRECTOR Sandy Kim
PHOTOGRAPHER Faith Mason
ILLUSTRATOR Rachel Ann Lindsay
FOOD STYLIST Kathryn Bruton
PROPS STYLIST Lydia Brun
PROJECT EDITOR Sophie Allen
EDITORIAL ASSISTANT Hannah Coughlin
PRODUCTION Nic Jones, Gemma John and Lisa Pinnell

Library of Congress Control Number: 2017938383
Colour reproduction by ALTA, London
Printed and bound in China by 1010 International Printing Ltd.

INTRODUCTION

Way back in 2009, over a few drinks with my dear friend Jane, I was intrigued by the concept of creating short recipes written in the style of a Twitter post. The idea posed an interesting challenge: could a recipe be delicious, inspiring and easy to follow using just 140 characters?

The 80 recipes on the following pages are fast, fun and easy, dispelling the notion that cooking can take too long or is too complicated. I hope they motivate you to spend a few quality minutes in the kitchen whipping them up—for a mid-week meal or a celebratory feast.

Use the recipes to inspire your culinary creativity. Trust your palate and don't be afraid to experiment. Most of all, have fun! Reaping the rewards of your efforts as you gather family and friends around the table is just so satisfying.

Andrea x

GLOSSARY

When the ingredients are listed consecutively with a specific measurement to start and commas separating the ingredients, use that measurement for each of the ingredients listed; e.g., "Mix 2T smkd paprika,lemzest olv oil" means "2 tablespoons" of each smoked paprika, lemon zest and olive oil, not a combined total of 2 tablespoons. When garlic is mentioned, unless specified otherwise, it refers to finely chopped garlic. Herbs are always fresh unless otherwise stated. "Serves 1, 2 or many" means that you can multiply the recipe to serve however many people you want. Below are the short forms used in the recipes.

& = and

+ = add

=parts = equal parts

~ = approximately

½'d = halved

¼'d = quartered

2 = to

almnd = almond

avo = avocado

b.pwdr = baking powder

bl ppr = black pepper

bl = black

blendr = blender

br.sugar = brown sugar

buttr = butter

C = cup

cauliflwr = cauliflower

centr = center

cinmon - cinnamon

chix = chicken

choc = chocolate

chop'd = chopped

cocnut = coconut

cookd = cooked

cran = cranberry

crushd = crushed

cvr = cover

Dijon = Dijon mustard

ea = each

EVOO = extra virgin olive oil

frsh = fresh

frzn = frozen

gingr = ginger

crn syrp = light corn syrup

glzd = glazed

gr olives = green olives

gr8'd = grated

gr8 = grate

grilld = grilled

grlic = garlic

grlicpwdr = garlic powder

grnd = ground

guac = guacamole

H2O = water

in2 = into

lemjuice = lemon juice

lemzest = lemon zest

marin8 = marinate

mozz = mozzarella

olv oil = olive oil

opn = open

ornge = orange

ovenprf = ovenproof

ovr = over

Parm = Parmesan

pc = pieces

pepprs = peppers

pickld = pickled

pnut = peanut

pots = potatoes

prk = pork

pwdr = powder

rst'd = roasted

S&P = salt and pepper

sesme = sesame

shred = shredded

simmr = simmer

slcd = sliced

smkd = smoked

scllns = scallions

srv = serve

sw.pot = sweet potato

T = tablespoon

t = teaspoon

tendr = tender

tog = together

tom = tomato

uncovrd = uncovered

v. = very

van = vanilla extract

vin = vinegar

w/ = with

wh wine = white wine

wht vin = white wine vinegar

whiskd = whisked

whiz = whizz or purée or blend

Worcest = Worcestershire sauce

BREAKFASTS & BRUNCH

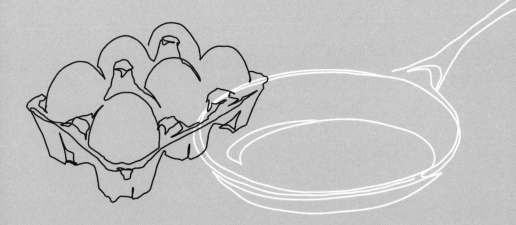

BR.SUGAR BACON

Mix ½lb slcd bacon w/½C br.sugar in sealable bag. Refrigerate ovr night. Transfer 2 foil-lined pan w/ rack&cook~350F, til crispy

EGGNHOLE

Buttr sides of sliced brioche, fry 1 side,flip,cut hole in centr&crack egg in2 hole.Flip 2 finish, eat w/crispy round 2 dip in2 egg

RASPBERRY REFRESH

Makes
1

PRETTY IN PINK SMOOTHIE

Whiz in blendr ¾C frozen raspberries, ¾C fresh apple juice, 1t grated ginger, pinch cinnamon

CROISSANT PERDU

Whisk 2eggs,⅓C milk, pinch nutmeg. Dunk stale croissants,
fry,med hot pan w/knob buttr til crispy. Warm maple syrup 2 srv

BREAKFAST TARTINE

Spread generous layer
ricotta on sourdough
toast, sprinkle w/
chop'd pistachios
(or fave nuts) & drizzle
w/best honey

SPEEDY SCONES

Mix 1¼C (heaped) flour, ¼C sugar, 2t b.pwdr.
Gr8 in 4T cold buttr+⅔C milk,3T currants,
shape round loaf on tray,425F~20/25min

SPARKLING MELON

Scoop melon balls&divide in glasses.
Pour generously prosecco ovr melon. Whiz
=parts frsh mint w/sugar, sprinkle 2 srv

FRUIT & NUT SMOOTHIE

Whiz fave frozen fruit in blender w/handful
whole almonds, 1T tahini & almond milk til smooth

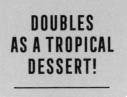

TROPICAL SALSA

Dice 1 mango,papaya, ½ pineapple.
Mix w/zest&juice1lime, 2 passionfruit, 1T honey,
chop'd mint, 1t gr8'd gingr, eat w/yogurt

MEDITERRANEAN AVO TOAST

Pat dry&fry 2T capers in 2T oil.
Toast 2 slices multigrain bread, top w/slcd avo,
crumbled feta, capers & oregano

CAULIFLWR CHORIZO HASH

Fry high heat chorizo&chop'd onion.
+cauliflwr florets&diced sw.pots,cook til tendr,
+handful spinach,top w/poach egg

MUSTARD GLZD SAUSAGES

Roast 6 sausages, turning 2 cook evenly.
Mix 3T ea Dijon,honey &brush
on sausages, cooking through til golden

CREAMY RADISH BAGEL

Mix 1t garlic, 10 gr8'd radishes, 8oz creamcheese, zest&juice 1 lime,2T chop'd parsley.Chill. Spread on toasted bagels

SOUPS
& SALADS

RED PEPPER SOUP

Sweat 1C chop'd onion,1t grlic. +28oz can toms,
5 rst'd red pepprs,4C veg stock,S&P,simmr~25min.
Purée. Top w/ornge zest

MEATBALL PHO

Brown meatballs w/2 chop'd scllns
&1T gr8'd gingr +3C chix stock&simmr. Add generous
handful each cookd rice noodles & spinach

CORN SOUP

Serves 4–6

ADD FRIED CHORIZO FOR A SPANISH TWIST

Sauté 1C ea chop'd leek,celery
+1T ea grlic,paprika.+1lb frzn corn,
cvr w/stock,simmr~30min,purée.
Top w/fried onions 2 srv

SW.POT PNUT SOUP

Sweat 1chop'd onion,1T grlic w/2t garam
masala.+4C sw.pot,2C carrot(chop'd),6C
stock,simr til tndr. Whiz w/4T pnutbuttr.S&P

ZUCCHINI CARPACCIO

Peel long strips of yellow/green zucchini. Plate&dress
w/=parts lemjuice/EVOO.
Top w/shaved Parm, fresh basil, S&P

TZATZIKI WEDGES

Mix 1C tzatziki w/gr8'd radish,chop'd oregano&thyme.
Cut iceberg in 6 wedges.
Dress w/tzatziki,garnish w/more radish,bl.ppr

CELERY ORANGE SALAD

Dice ½lb celery,sauté w/1T coriander,
remove heat, + 1T ea gr8'd ginger,
ornge zest,whitebalsamic,EVOO. S&P

CARROT CRAN SLAW

Mix ¾lb julienne carrot w/2t cumin seeds,
3T ea dried cranberries,pumpkin seeds,chop'd
parsley/cilantro,limejuice,EVOO.S&P

PEACHY
BURRATA

Combine generous
handful arugula,+
torn pieces of burrata,
grilled peach wedges.
Drizzle w/EVOO.S&P

JEWELLED FREEKEH

Mix 3C cookd freekeh w/2 oranges (zest,segments juice), 3T gr olives, 4T pomegranate seeds, ½C feta. Drizzle EVOO. S&P

TAHINI-MINT PICNIC POTATOES

Whisk 1t dried mint, 2T lemjuice,
¼C ea tahini,mayo,yogurt. Toss w/1½lbs cookd
new pots, chop'd parsley,mint,S&P

GINGR
TUNA SALAD

Mix 4T chop'd pickld gingr,rice vin&2T mirin,oil.
+jar quality tuna(drain),1t bl sesme seeds,1scallion.
Srv w/avo&pea shoots

ALWAYS A WINNING COMBO

Serves 1, 2 or many

BLT BOWL

Mix cherry tom halves, gem lettuce, crispy pancetta, chunky croutons. Drizzle w/EVOO & balsamic.S&P

SUPERFAST
SUPPERS

MARGHERITA MUFFIN

Split English muffin, toast&spread w/tom sauce,
torn buffalo mozz, ½'d cherry toms. Grill til melted.
Top w/basil. S&P

PARSLEY PESTO PASTA

Whiz 2cloves grlic, bunch parsley,
¼C ea walnuts,olv oil&gr8'd Parm.
Toss w/1lb cookd linguini & 1t chile flakes

ZESTY PASTA

Toss 1lb cookd angel hair pasta w/zest
4 lemons, ¾C gr8'd Parm, 2t bl ppr.
Drizzle EVOO, sprinkle w/crunchy breadcrumbs

DELICIOUS
HOT OR COLD

*Serves
4-6*

SUMMER PASTA

Mix 1pint ½'d cherry toms, 8oz feta,1t grlic,¾C EVOO,
1t S&P. Cvr&marin8 2 hrs. +1lb cookd pasta,
¼C gr8'd Parm&frsh basil

MOLLUSK MIX

Sauté 1t grlic w/1T gr8'd gingr,3T olv oil.
+1lb ea mussels,clams,1C wh wine,cvr,med-high,
til shells opn.+5T cream,parsley

GROUPER MEDALLIONS

Brush grouper w/olv oil, S&P.
Sprinkle generously w/za'atar,bake ~10min,finish
w/ornge zest. Srv w/herby couscous

FISH STICK TACOS

Place 1 cookd fish
stick in soft taco,
garnish w/avo slices,
¼'d cherry toms, top
w/plain yogurt
& cilantro

MR JAY JAY'S SWEET CRUST SALMON

Brush ea salmon fillet (skin-side down)
w/olv oil&2t Dijon. Sprinkle w/2t br.sugar. S&P.
Bake 350F~10mins

JUNIPER TUNA

Heat 1T olv oil,juniper berries w/rosemary/sage
sprigs.+2 tuna steaks,sear high heat.
Flip,+2T balsamic, juice&segments 1 ornge

MEXI-BURGER

Mix 1lb ea ground prk&beef w/2T fajita seasoning. Shape 6
patties, grill. Toast buns, top w/salsa, avo, sour cream & jalapenos

FAB FRENCH CHIX

Brush 4 chix breasts skin on w/olv oil.
Squeeze lemjuice ovr, sprinkle w/dried
tarragon&paprika. Roast 350F uncovrd~30min

A VERSATILE RUB!
TRY ON SHRIMP
OR PORK

Serves
4

MASALA ORNGE DUCK

Mix 1T ea garam masala,sesame seeds,½t ea grlic pwdr,grnd gingr,2T ea ornge juice/zest,EVOO. Brush ovr 4 cookd duck breasts

EASY APRICOT CHIX

Brush 1C apricot jam ovr 2lbs chix thighs/drumstix,
bake 350F uncovrd~45mins/1hr til fully cooked.
Serve w/creamy polenta

FIGGY PIGGY

Brown 4 prk loin chops. Set aside. Fry 1 slcd onion.
Stir in 4T ea fig&plum jams&grainy mustard,H2O.
Add chops, fry ~5/10mins.S&P

EASY ENTERTAINING

SHRIMP GUAC

Mash 2 avo, ¼t ea grlic,chile flakes,salt
+2T ea lime juice,cilantro. Mix in ¼lb chop'd cookd
shrimp. Srv w/tortilla chips

FETA DIP

Whiz 8oz feta w/½C ea ricotta & rst'd red pepprs, 2T lemjuice,
splash EVOO+1t ea fresh thyme,oregano &chile flakes

AVO&WHITE BEAN DIP

Whiz 1can cannellini beans,1 avo, ½t garlic, handful
fresh parsley, 4T ea lemjuice,EVOO. Season w/sea salt

WARM ARTICHOKE DIP

Drain&pulse 1can artichoke hearts w/1C ea mayo, gr8'd Parm,
¼t grlic pwdr,2T parsley. Ovenprf dish, bake 350F~45min

KALE CHIPS

Coat kale leaves w/olv oil. S&P. Lay on baking
sheet, no overlap. Bake&shake to ensure
even cooking 400F~9min

GOOEY
GOODNESS

Serves
4

FONTINA
FONDU

Gr8 6oz Fontina cheese in 9in castiron pan.
Top w/sliced grlic,chile flakes,rosemary,S&P,
broil til bubbly. Srv w/bread

FENNEL
TAPENADE

Slice fennel bulb,toss w/oil,
S&P,roast400F~20mins.
Pulse w/2T pinenuts,¼C gr olives,
1T ea capers,parsley,grlic,
lemzest&EVOO

PICKLED ONIONS

Pour boiling H2O ovr v. thinly slcd red onions, drain & place in jar. Cvr w/white wine vin, ½t ea salt,sugar. Rest 1 hour

STILTON PATÉ

Pulse in food processor ½C ea blue cheese,cream cheese &buttr w/1t bl ppr, chill. Srv w/water crackers & v. thinly sliced pear

Serves 6-8

SIMPLE STUNNING CANAPÉ

SAGE
HOT
BREAD

Slice baguette. Blend
4T saltd buttr
w/zest of 1 lemon&
1t dried sage. Buttr ea
slice,reshape loaf,wrap
w/foil&warm 2 srv

**Makes
1**

**ADD ROSEMARY
FOR HERBY
FLAVOR**

SOCCA

Whisk 1C chickpea
flour,½C H2O,
2T olv oil,1t salt.
Rest 60min. Heat
2T oil 2 smoke,lrg
pan, pour battr, bake
500F~15min til goldn

BLACK OLIVE DIP

Whiz ⅓C bl olives,
1anchovy,1t ea capers,grlic,
1Tparsley+¼C EVOO.
Add 1T ea redwine vin,
lemjuice & season w/bl ppr

ASPARAGUS
BUNDLES

Wrap tog middle section 3
asparagus w/prosciutto,repeat.
Roast 375F ~15mins til tendr,
sprinkle w/gr8'dParm,
bake 2mins

GRILLED ENDIVE

Split endive in ½ lengthwise, lightly oil,S&P.
Grill til charred&tendr. Top w/Gorgonzola, grill.
Drizzle w/balsamic&EVOO

CAVOLO NERO &BURRATA

Sauté cavolo nero w/slcd grlic til tendr.
Portion in pan,top w/torn burrata,cvr 2 warm,
drizzle w/EVOO. S&P

FIRE UP
THE Q!

Serves
2

SOY GLAZE PORK

Marin8 2 pork chops, 4hrs in 6T soy,
2T ea H2O&br.sugar, dash Worcest, 2crushd grlic.
BBQ, baste w/sauce, srv w/sw.pot fries

FIRE SHRIMP

Melt 2T buttr,sriracha, slcd grlic, med-high heat.
+12 shell-on jumbo shrimp,cook~5min til pink.
Srv w/chop'd parsley,lemon wedges

TANDOORI LAMB CUTLETS

Mix ½C tandoori paste w/½C plain yogurt.
Add 1lb lamb cutlets,marin8 24hrs. Best on grill
or broil hot oven

TZATZIKI

Mix ½C gr8'd cucumber, ½C plain yogurt,
1 clove chop'd grlic, 1t dried mint,
1t lemjuice. S&P

Serves
4

MEDITERRANEAN
MOTHER SAUCE

SMOKY BEEF SKEWERS

Mix 2T ea smkd paprika,lemzest,olv oil
w/1T ea grlic,dried mint.S&P. Rub in2
1lb cubed beef,marin8 ovrnight.Skewer&grill

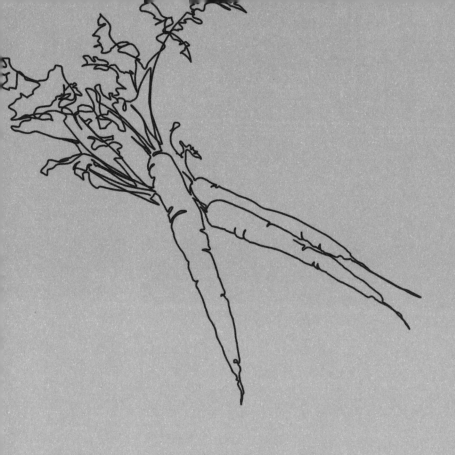

SIMPLE
SIDES

ALSO USE AS A
SMOKY STEAK
BUTTER

*Makes
6*

CORN & SMKD PAPRIKA BUTTER

Mix 1t smkd paprika w/4T soft salted buttr.
Grill or boil 6 corn cobs. Spread w/buttr
& garnish w/cilantro

SMASHED CELERIAC

Peel&chop celeriac,cvr
w/vegstock,simmr til soft
~15mins, drain,mash w/
1T buttr, 1C cookd bulgur, 1T
chop'd parsley. S&P

A NEW TAKE ON MASH

Serves
4-6

FAMILY-STYLE TABLE STATEMENT

Serves a crowd

VEGGIE TIAN

Layer =prts slcd toms,zucchini,
onion&eggplant in rows,
ovenprf dish.Season w/
herbes de Provence,S&P&olv oil.
Bake~350F til soft

**EASY &
IMPRESSIVE**

*Serves 1, 2 or
many*

MOM'S
BLUECHEESE TOMS

Season thick slcd toms w/S&P,sugar&dried basil.
Mix 1T ea breadcrumbs,bluecheese per tom,
top toms,bake 350F til golden

**TRY SALT
BAKING
WHOLE FISH**

*Serves
4-6*

SALTBAKED
BEETS

Mix 2lbs kosher salt,3 whiskd egg wht,¼C H2O,
5staranise,zest 1ornge. Ovenprf dish,lay
6beets,cvr w/salt mix,bake~1hr,350F

GREEN BEANS GREMOLATA

Mix 2T chop'd parsley, zest 2 lemons,
1T EVOO, ¼t grlic. Toss w/
½lb blanched green beans. S&P

TOSS IN A
SPINACH SALAD

Serves 4

BALSAMIC
BUTTONS

Toss 8oz button
mushrooms w/3T
EVOO,5T balsamic,
S&P. Roast 400F,
shallow pan w/sprigs
rosemary~20mins

EGGPLANT BOATS

Toast 1T caraway, cumin,coriander. Whiz w/12oz rst'd red peppr, 2t chile flakes.Spread on grilld eggplant, top w/Parm,warm

Makes
1¼ cups sauce

MIX LEFTOVER SAUCE WITH YOGURT FOR A DIP

CHERRY TOM BAKE

Whiz 2 pc bread,¼C gr8'd Parm,1T parsley,
2T EVOO,1t grlic. Halve 1lb cherry toms in ovenprf dish,
top w/crumb,bake350F~20min

STICKY CARROTS

10oz young carrots in large pan w/1T sugar,
2T buttr+½C H2O. Simmr cvrd 5mins,
uncover&cook til sticky. Finish w/sea salt

CRISPY POTS

Boil new pots til tendr,drain. Lay on baking sheet,crush gently w/back of spoon.Toss w/olv oil,sea salt, roast hot oven til crispy

SWEET
ENDINGS

AFFOGATO

Take 2 scoops of very best vanilla
ice cream & drown w/shot of hot espresso

CHEESECAKE TART

Whisk 8oz cream cheese,1/4C sugar,1t lemjuice,1egg.
Fill 9in pie shell,bake 325F~30min 2 set,cool.
Spread jam ovr top 2 srv

BOOZY BERRY FOOL

Pour splash of Cointreau ovr berries. Cover, leave 1hr (or more). Spoon ovr crushd meringue,top w/whipped cream,fresh mint

PNUT BRITTLE CRUNCH ICE CREAM

Crush 1/2C pnut brittle&fold in2
1pint slightly softened vanilla ice cream.
Re-freeze, sprinkle w/brittle 2 sv

DEB'S CHOC DELIGHT

Cream 2 sticks buttr, 2C sugar,4T cocoa.
+4 eggs, 1C flour. Bake in greased pan,350F~25mins.
Dust w/conf sugar

ALMND
BONBONS

Mix ⅔C almnd buttr w/2C Rice Krispies,
2T maple syrup&pinch salt. Drop by T in
unsweetened shred cocnut,roll balls,chill

COCONUT RICE PUD

Simmr 1C basmati,2C H2O,cinmon stick~10min
+2C cocnut milk,4T sugar~15mins.
Srv w/generous chop'd nuts&dried fruit

BR.SUGAR
TARTS

Beat 4T buttr,½C br.sugar,corn syrp.
Stir in 1egg, 1t ea van,lemjuice,wht vin,salt.
Fill mini tart shells,bake350F,15 min

GROWNUP SUNDAE

Heat ½C maple syrup
w/½T buttr+2T brandy.
Cool. Pour ovr very
best vanilla ice cream&
garnish w/chop'd walnuts

INDEX

ACKNOWLEDGMENTS

Massive thanks first and foremost to Kyle Cathie, my publisher and Sophie Allen, editor extraordinare! Thank you for sharing my vision and for your patience in what became a very fast-moving project. I feel very lucky to have had such expertise and guidance on this book and hope this is the first of many.

Sandy Kim, I don't even have words to put to paper to express how happy I was the second you said "yes." Your creative amazingness, dedication and friendship have taken this book from good to great – thank you!

Faith Mason, Kathryn Bruton and Lydia Brun, thank you for your hard work, collaboration and talent. From the get-go I said this project needed a special team and you all stepped up to the challenge and delivered.

I am hugely grateful to my friend Jane Francisco – without you this idea (and a few of the recipes) may have just never come about. Thank you for continuing to believe in me and always pushing me to take that next step.

To my recipe testers, Kelly Richardson and Jenny Dulmage, I will be forever indebted to you for your willingness, enthusiasm and honest feedback. Mom, Rony Zibara, Jason Campbell, Deby Taylor, Elaine Clark and Lynn Johnston – thank you for sharing your recipes – they made it!

Gigi Morin and Doug Wallace, you dotted the i's, crossed the t's and I will always be appreciative for your individual areas of expertise and willingness to always help me, no questions asked.

Last but not least, thank you to my husband Michael Clark and Oxford, who never left my side throughout this journey nor complained about repeatedly eating the same recipe over and over. Your endless support goes unmatched. xx